I Found the Answer

Peace be
your journey
Paula
2014

Rosita Hall

I Found The Answer

Do you want to live a less stressful and more joyful life?

Epic
Press

Belleville, Ontario, Canada

I Found the Answer

Copyright © 2003, Rosita Hall

First printing, December 2003
Second printing, May 2004
Third printing, January 2006
Fourth printing, March 2009
Fifth printing, May 2011
Sixth printing, November 2012

National Library of Canada Cataloguing in Publication

Hall, Rosita, 1959-
I found the answer : do you want to live a less stressful and more joyful life? / Rosita Hall.

ISBN 978-1-55306-641-5

1. Self-realization. I. Title.

BF637.S4H28 2003   158.1   C2003-905935-9

Also available as an e-book from Kindle, KOBO and the iBookstore

**For more information or
to order additional copies, please contact:**

Rosita Hall
P.O. Box 57028, Jackson Station
Hamilton, ON L8P 4W9
(905) 521-7329

Epic Press is an imprint of *Essence Publishing,* a Christian Book Publisher dedicated to furthering the work of Christ through the written word. For more information, contact:
20 Hanna Court, Belleville, Ontario, Canada K8P 5J2.
Phone: 1-800-238-6376 • Fax: (613) 962-3055.
E-mail: info@essence-publishing.com
Website: www.essence-publishing.com

To my husband, Norm,
whom I love with all my heart and soul!

The body is an incredible gift from God. Only He could create such a wonder. I show my unwavering gratitude to Him every day by choosing to take care of mine.

—*Rosita*

Acknowledgements

This book would not be possible without God, from whom all blessings flow...thank you, God.

To Norman, my husband, and best friend: thank you for your inspiration, support, patience, and undying enthusiasm, from the beginning to the completion of this book. You are an amazing husband and father, and indeed, the wind beneath my wings. Much love and respect!

To Kathy Glover Scott: thank you for being brave enough to send me back to the drawing board, and for your wonderful ideas and suggestions!

To Fanny, Fran, Pat, and Brenda: thank you for reading my very first draft, and for your words of encouragement, and support of my endeavors.

To my two little men, Joshua and Christian: thank you for always being Mom's faithful cheerleaders. I love you very much!

I would also like to extend a word of thanks to the various supporters who encouraged me to write this book.

Last, but not least, to my dear friend Rosita Perez, retired professional speaker extraordinaire, who has always encouraged me to be myself, and said that success would follow: thank you in a big, big way!

May God bless you all,
Rosita

Preface

The human body, soul, and spirit have always fascinated me. Have you ever considered the magnitude, and the array of intricacies, that take place in our bodies with each breath that we take? This is all due to the fine workmanship of God. He is the custom designer, and has tailored-made each and every one of us in awesome ways. I am in constant awe of how beautifully He has equipped us for this journey of life that we have been called upon to take. I know with my deepest convictions that God has created both you and me in this magnificent way to enable us to become missionaries of His will. We are phenomenal creatures, and God knew exactly what He was doing when He created each beautiful temple. We have been placed on this earth to do service with God.

I am fascinated by the art of self-care, because I know that I cannot do God's work unless I am taking care of myself completely. This means that I need to nurture my mental, spiritual, physical, and emotional self, while having constant communion with God, as He holds the power that I need to make this happen.

As you journey through the pages of this book, understand that God is, and always has been, a stabilizing force in my life. I believe that you and I are incredibly gifted and can become the people God has created us to be, by taking care of ourselves and realizing the full potential God sees and places in us.

There are several references in this book where I refer to tapping into our internal resources, and getting connected to self and our internal abundance. Please note that this has happened to me because of my unwavering faith in the One who created each and every one of us; and that I am able to do so because I am in constant communion with God, seeking His wisdom and truth. I ask for His guidance, strength, and encouragement, and I give daily thanks for His blessings. My self and spiritual awareness is an ongoing process, and one where I will always be walking in unison with God. Unravelling our gifts and reaching a new level of awareness and spiritual renewal is a process that is available to everyone, if we acknowledge God and give praise to Him for making it all possible.

Introduction

According to my parents and my siblings, I was, and still continue to be, different from the rest of the clan. I certainly put the 'you' in unique.

I was always the one to choose the road less travelled, and I always marched to the beat of a different drum. This made me question, "Am I really a member of this family?" The answer was, "yes," indeed I was.

I believe that my Mom owned the copyright to the nursery rhyme, "There was an old woman who lived in a shoe," (except my mother never appeared old to me.) I am one of fourteen children: eight brothers and five sisters, to be exact. Needless to say, from my perspective, most times our home seemed like Grand Central Station with all of the comings and goings.

Even as a child I needed an escape from reality every once in a while; a way to tune out the noise, confusion, and steady pace. At a very young age, I was able to connect with my inner self, a haven which I now refer to as "The Land Down Under," where I would retreat to find quiet, serenity, and calm.

According to my mother, at an early age I loved to be by myself, and I also loved having conversations with myself. My mother said sometimes she would hear excessive talking coming from a room in the house, and she would think it was me with a group of my friends or other siblings, but when she walked in, to her surprise it was only "me, myself and I." At other times, I could be found sitting quietly, as if meditating. I also liked to sing and dance, and I was basically a happy, and normal child. Those particular memories I shall hold on to forever, for they are a part of my *foundation,* the very essence of who I am, what I am becoming, and how I came to be so passionate about the issues of self-care. I want to thank my mother for not calling the men in the white coats (the doctors), because many people would think that any child having excessive conversations with him/herself or meditating, or journeying within, would definitely need a therapeutic assessment, or some quick-fix medication. How can a five-year-old kid journey to the "Land Down Under?" Well, let me tell you, it's been done!

You see, what I understand now as an adult, is that, as a young child, I was already making that connection to the internal self and utilizing my internal resources, without really understanding what was going on. I certainly remember feeling happy, and I remember my times alone and feeling wonderful about an internal peacefulness and joy I was feeling. What I didn't understand then, is that somehow, and in some magical and spiritual way, I was able to open the gift that was given to me to use on my journey called life.

From the moment we take our first breath, we are blessed, and are given an abundance of internal resources. It is a gift from God; the survival kit we need to support us on this journey. I truly have been blessed, because somehow, I managed to tap into mine at an incredibly young age. I am of the belief that this is indeed the crucial time when we are truly called to unwrap this special gift. Unfortunately for many, this experience does not begin until we become adults, and then the process becomes more difficult because it is often tainted or layered with life's battle wounds, or preconceptions about who we are and what we are expected to be. Without the right support systems and determination, one may never have the opportunity to cash in on his/her million dollar resources. Forget television's "Who Wants To Be A Millionaire?" You already are one; you just haven't gone to the bank to cash in on all of your internal wealth.

I must be clear about the fact that having these resources does not make you a saint or immune to life's struggles, disappointments, setbacks, bad choices, and grief along the way—but neither does the million dollars offered on a game show. What these resources do, is enable you to bounce back and move forward, no matter what cards are dealt to you.

My ability to connect with my internal self at such an early age, and my ability to continuously draw upon my million dollar resources, have given me the ability to love God first, then myself, and then to spiritually connect with others. As a result, I have affected many lives and because of that, my life has been truly blessed.

I have often been called an angel by friends, and complete strangers, alike. Who knows, maybe I am an angel, but the secret is simply that my love radiates, and it's so natural for me to give to others without much thought. That's what happens when you give to God first. It then makes it so easy to give to others! An outpour of love and kindness is just an automatic response. If you meet me for the first time and I hug you, please know that I'm just doing what comes naturally to me—sharing the gift of life and love!

The magic truly comes from an ability to discover God's heaven from within; to embrace love, respect who we are, access our powerhouse of boundless resources, and to discard each and every thing that is not nurturing our hearts and souls. It also comes from having faith in a higher being, and having faith in ourselves. A line from Shakespeare's Hamlet says it all: "to thine own self be true." That is really what this book is all about. It's about teaching you how to love yourself first, and care for yourself, so you can give two-fold to others. It's about embracing the "you" in uniqueness, understanding your past, embracing the future, and living each day as if it were your last; about not getting caught up in all the 'stuff' in life that makes us feel unworthy and inadequate.

My mother, the survivor of raising fourteen children to adulthood, was a woman of amazing faith. She always had a song in her heart, and she would sing so passionately about faith and her belief in God. I often listened as she sang one song in particular entitled, "I Found the Answer." She clung to that song of faith during some of her darkest and most challenging times as a daughter, wife, and mother. When I embarked upon the project of writing this book, many titles flowed through my mind, but "I Found the Answer" settled itself firmly and quietly in my psyche, and refused to move. It's simply because I truly have found the answer to a fulfilling and loving lifestyle. The journey began in 1959 when a wonderful woman gave birth to me through God's love.

With love,
Rosita

A Special Note to My Readers

The greatest endowment that we could ever entrust to ourselves, is the *time* and the *courage* required to embrace and understand who we are, in our entire splendour; and to utilize our abilities, gifts, and talents that were given to us by God on the day that we were born.

We often struggle unnecessarily in our day-to-day activities simply because we haven't realized the magnitude of our true potential, or taken the time to discover who we are in our entirety. We fail to utilize our most powerful resource, which is the *self,* through God. God is our most powerful resource. He is our survival kit; a critical resource that is required on this journey called life.

Not only do we need to understand who we are and utilize our untapped *"self"* in its entirety; we also need to learn how to *care* for ourselves, and thus our resources, so that they are functioning when we need them the most. When *"self"* is malfunctioning, or not operating at peak performance, we set ourselves up for stress, stress, and more stress.

Are you overworked, overwhelmed, or tired? Is your life spinning out of control? Is work making you crazy? Has change got you in a noose? Need an emotional or mental tune-up? Perhaps some 'me' time? Then you've picked up the right book. I want to inspire and encourage you to be the best you can be, by showing you how to discover your untapped internal resources through a process of *self awareness* and *self-care,* and help you *recognize how awesomely equipped you are.* You have enough internal firearms to get you through any of life's tough spots, and can lead a more joyful, healthful, and purposeful life.

Finally, I want to inspire you to live life to the fullest by paying attention to the small blessings that surround us. I want you to come to terms with some of life's inevitabilities, such as aging, death, and some of the other "stuff" that keeps us awake at night. May the pages you are about to read silence the noise and clutter, turn on your heart light, lead you to the path of inner wisdom, and awaken you to boundless possibilities.

Rosita

"*I may not be the most skilled or efficient home builder, but one thing I know for sure is that whatever home I build, it better be standing on a solid foundation.*"

Rosita

There's no Place like Home...

Building a Solid Foundation

I am amazed at how quickly undeveloped land can turn into a neighborhood, sprouting new luxurious homes, trees, sidewalks, and people in just a matter of what seems like days. Isn't this process supposed to take longer? We live in a society where we demand expediency. Our need for a quick fix doesn't exclude the building of the family home, which will probably be one of the biggest financial investments in our lifetime.

Recently I watched as some new homes sprouted up in my neighborhood. I set out on my daily jogging excursions, keeping a close eye on the construction from beginning to end; the amount of progress made from day to day simply astounded me. Those guys really worked fast! In no time at all, another stream of houses would be ready. I often wondered about the craftsmanship and the quality of what looked perfect from the outside.

Watching the entire process brought me back to my childhood, as I remembered the tale of three little homebuilders I use to read about. Remember the *Three Little Pigs?* Those were the guys who had to build their homes very quickly because the big bad wolf was hot on their heels. Well, they certainly had motivation to get the job done quickly. What's our motivation for getting the job done so quickly? Who's hot on our heels? Why do we need everything done yesterday? Is it because we validate our worth as human beings by the size of our homes, the cars we drive, and our bank accounts? What price are we willing to pay for this kind of validation?

Can we really afford the luxurious homes we are buying? If not, why do some of us choose to stress ourselves to the max, sacrificing our health to pay for them, furnish them, and do the regular upkeep? As if that's not enough to send us close to the edge emotionally and financially, how about the cars we need to go with the fancy houses? By the way, is the two-car garage really just for show? After all, why would we want our $45,000 car sitting in the garage? We need to have it on display. We need validation, remember? So, our garages quickly turn into additional storage space. What's up with that?

The bottom line is this: If you can afford it, and it's not draining you emotionally, mentally and spiritually, more power to you. If you can't, then living large is going to cause you some financial woes and an even higher price to pay in regards to your emotional and physical health. Is it worth it?

I became fascinated with the art of home building and our desire to have it all, a few years ago, when I came to the realization that I needed to do an inspection of my own home, and consider some remodeling, remolding, and maintenance on the home that I built. Yes, you heard me right, the one that I built.

My home, however, was not constructed in a matter of days or months. It was built from the inside out, not the outside in, and has taken me some forty-odd years to get the foundation standing sturdily enough to hold up the rest of the structure. Every good builder knows a solid foundation is critical.

To some, my home could be viewed as interesting and unique in appearance, and actually pretty average in size, measuring at about 5' 8" in height, medium framed, and very unassuming from the exterior. But don't let the size fool you, because the foundation is as solid as a rock—sturdy enough to brave any kind of weather; and you really should check out the interior—top-notch stuff inside.

You see, it's the life that we build for ourselves on the *inside* that is our **real** home. Homebuilding starts on the inside, where the heart is, and where the spirit thrives, and it requires a lot of emotional and mental labour. It doesn't require bricks and mortar, and certainly can't be constructed in a matter of days, or weeks. Instead, it requires an ongoing lifetime process of trial and error, with regards to the *choices* we make or don't make, the *company we keep, life experiences,* our *upbringing, relationships we build along the way,* and most importantly, *our relationship with self.* Are we willing to invest as much time and effort in ourselves as we are in building and maintaining our luxurious family homes? What commitments are you prepared to make today to yourself to ensure that this happens?

Building from within is a process that requires careful crafts-manship and regular self-maintenance, so that it can survive heartache, separation, divorce, death, loss of job, or any of life's big bad wolves that we must come face-to-face with; our foundation will be **oh, so solid**!

My home building experience started in a fashion similar to that of the *Three Little Pigs.* Initially, I was building my **real** home in a hurry without a sense of clarity, direction, and purpose; and so, like the first and second little piggies, my home didn't stand the test of time, or the storms of life—but that all occurred when I was still new to the business of personal growth and self development. Now, with experience under my belt, I could be described as a well-sea-soned expert in the art of **real** home building. I now know what it takes to keep my foundation, which is essentially my life, strong and well grounded. It takes a tremendous amount of self-care, soul searching, and courage, to be the real me. Please understand that having such a foundation doesn't keep life's struggles and demons away from us. Remember the third little pig's brick house was solid, but that didn't keep the big bad wolf away. What it does do how-ever, is equip us with the strength and courage we need to get through tough times and deal with situations head-on without destroying ourselves.

What kind of foundation is your house standing on? Do you rec-ognize the landscape, which is the 'self', after a life storm? Take some time to do an inspection of your own internal home and the foun-dation that makes it what it is. Does it provide you with the comfort and security that every good home should? If not, then maybe it's time that we rewrite our own version of *The Three Little Pigs* that would include a fourth piggy who doesn't just focus on building material things, but also understands and appreciates that our biggest investment of a lifetime should be in the building, ongoing maintenance, and nurturance of our internal havens; which includes our emotional, mental, physical and spiritual self. Remember, your health is your wealth! Now that's a smart investment. No financial commitment are required, and the returns are unbelievable. Get ready! Get set! Get prepared, because you never know when you might hear "*little pig, little pig, let me come in; or I'll huff and I'll puff, and I'll blow your house in.*"

I can never hide from myself. Wherever I go, there I am. This is why self-awareness is a critical component in the building and maintenance of our internal havens.

—*Rosita*

Finding Me...

Miracles unfold even in darkness. It's not always the light to which we should look for our strength and to hear God's Messages.

—Rosita

I was led to the doorway of self-awareness in 1983. I nearly missed this amazing opportunity because it came to me cleverly disguised as death. It brought me to The Land Down Under which is my authentic self.

In a five-year-span, I lost a father, a mother, two grandmothers, and a great grandmother to death's call. The people I loved were leaving me in a way that could only be described as a domino effect. I felt empty, alone, and as if a piece of me had died as well. I tried desperately to make sense out of all these deaths, but to no avail. All I could think of was that I was losing my history, my connection to the past, the foundation to my future, and my stability. I was being robbed of my very own existence. Was my life story over? Could I carry on? Would I be next? How could I prepare for the next scene in my life or the next chapter, without them? It wouldn't be easy. I wrestled with many feelings, cried a lot, and started searching for deeper meaning. Somehow, I knew I had to make sense of it all. I had to silence the demons and their toxic talk that stirred so viciously inside, so I could hear God's messages.

What I soon discovered, after some serious soul searching and inner cleansing, was that through each death, God was bringing me closer to my *authentic self*. He was extending an invitation for me to truly meet that woman who stares back at me every day in the mirror. He was forcing me to now depend on my own powerhouse of resources, which I didn't realize I had, to guide me down the path of life. He was showing me that I really wasn't alone, and that all that I needed was *inside* of me. He was sending me a clear message, that on this journey called life, the roads won't always be paved with joy, and that I must use what He gave me at birth to overcome some of the hurdles.

I had constant flashbacks of how my mother, an amazing woman of faith, would always turn to the Creator for answers. Out of desperation, I opened my heart completely to God, and a transformation started taking place inside of me. I began to feel as though I was getting the *life scared into me!* I suppose you could call it my personal wake-up call. Little did I know that a whole new world was about to unravel for me. The process of self-awareness was unfolding, like a butterfly making its way out of its cocoon. The emptiness started to fade, and I began to feel the emergence of something inside that felt so right, and so alive, that I started experiencing some soulful energy, and it felt good. For the first time, I was discovering the real me, and all that I had inside of me through God's grace.

My faith continued to grow much stronger, and I understood clearly what the words "I will never leave you or forsake you" really meant. My heaven within exploded, and I got tuned into me, emotionally, mentally, physically, and spiritually. Wow, what a revelation! Yes folks, with God, we do indeed, have everything we need to get us through the many challenges and day-to-day struggles which we will all face. We just have to remember that the answers are all with God, on the inside, not on the outside.

What an absolutely amazing journey it has been, and continues to be, since I discovered this. My self-awareness journey has taught me that through God *I am powerful beyond my wildest dreams. I am in control of my thoughts and feelings, and every decision I make, or don't make, will affect my life,* and *nothing lasts forever.* My self-esteem skyrocketed, and while I was getting turned on to myself through God, people were getting turned on to me. That's how it works: people can't get turned on to you, until you can get turned on to yourself first! That can only happen if you take the time to discover who you really are and to define your purpose in life.

Until God took me on this journey, I didn't really know the authentic me, all that I had to offer, and all that I could be. I was also taught a big lesson about life which is this: When we become afraid and stagnated by what may look like darkness, if we keep our eyes open and focused on God, there will always be the dawning of a new day or a new beginning. The only way to do this is by coming up for air from all of your daily responsibilities, and paying a visit to 'self' through prayer, meditation, and conversation with God. When I came up for air and made a visit to the land of me, I learned that when the curtain falls on a certain part of your life, no matter how wonderful or how painful it is, it's over, and the next scene or chapter will begin if we allow it to. We must let go of what used to be in order to embrace what is.

Even though a chapter or scene in your life is over, it will always be a part of your life's story, a part of your history; but it can't be relived or brought back to life. I was stuck in a time warp trying to bring my past back into reality; but after experiencing the incredible amount of energy it took to do this, I started focusing on new chapters in my life. Through God's love and guidance, I came to understand that through God, I am now in charge, and it's my turn to leave a legacy for my children and grandchildren. I can have an incredible impact on my family history. It's too bad it takes losses like those I experienced in my life, to make many of us realize why we are on this journey called Life.

Death has taught me my greatest lesson in life. Death is now my friend, and as we dance together each and every day, her movements tell me over and over again that it's about more than work, big houses, over-extended credit, and stresses to the max. It's about that wonderful you who is waiting to unveil him/herself; utilizing your resources, nurturing those resources, and giving some of your energy and love to others.

The process of self-awareness is not a temporary mission; it's a commitment you make to yourself for a *lifetime* and it requires hard work, determination, and an attitude of *me first for a change.* Through this process, I was able to grasp what really matters in this awesomely magnificent universe.

Based on our individual experiences in life, and our reaction to these experiences, the things that matter in life will be different for each and every one of us. For me, it changes constantly on my journey, but finally, I feel comfortable with those things that matter the most to me at this very moment. For me, God matters, fresh flowers matter, a loving and caring husband matters, rain matters, sunshine matters, healthy friendships matter, my children matter, self-love matters, taking care of myself matters, waking to the dawning of a new day matters, morning tea with my two sons matters, the 10 p.m. episode of *Everybody loves Raymond* matters, my garden matters. All the other stuff I keep at a distance, because I don't care to own them, nor am I a slave to the "stuff" in life that triggers heart disease, unnecessary stress, guilt, anger, and so on. I've "been there, done that," and I've got the battle wounds to prove it. It's a life I can do without!

Reality check? Yes, I know that work, daily stresses, sickness, and death are all a part of life. I have not dismissed them as if they no longer exist or can no longer invade my space. It's just that I have chosen to no longer be consumed by them. I will not allow them to destroy my emotional, mental, and physical well-being. The only type of life I choose to live now is one filled with laughter, continued self-discovery, unconditional love for others, passion for those things that matter to me, and a loyalty and commitment to my God and then myself. I don't need a fancy home to measure my worth as a human being. I don't need a fancy car so that total strangers can gawk and admire it, to make me feel worthy. That's not how I define myself as a human being. Furthermore, I don't need to measure my success by my bank account. I don't need to measure my age by years, but rather by the number of hearts I've touched. My self-discovery journey has paved the path to a peace in my heart that passes all understanding, and because of that, I am truly "Living La Vida Loca." I've discovered who I really am, accepted my strengths and weaknesses, and, because of the gifts I was adorned with at birth, I now recognize that the world is at my feet with its amazing and boundless possibilities.

If Death hadn't come along and *scared the life into me,* I might still be at the same desk I started out at after graduating from university; at the same job, doing the exact same thing, still bathing in self-pity and never truly realizing or accessing my many talents and gifts. I had no idea that I was so talented and so awesomely equipped, until I got turned on to myself. It's easy to stay stuck and in the comfort zone. Trust me, I know that feeling. In my case, "The day came, when the risk it took to remain tight in the bud, became more painful than the risk it took to blossom" (*Anais Nin*).

I continue to take risks, and I continue to grow, blossom, and learn from the many challenges and opportunities I meet along the way. I am able to do this because I know I have a God-given safety net within me. I now take life by the lapel each and every day, and I challenge life, instead of the other way around. One doesn't need to ask me, "How's life treating you?" but rather, "How are you treating life?" What a truly exciting journey this can be. Oh, how I love life and I want the same for you!

When Death does come knocking on my door, I want to be singing *I Had The Time Of My Life,* because that's the song my heart keeps playing over and over again. What song will your heart be singing when your time comes?

Death is not the enemy. She is not a dark cloud hovering over us. She is Life, and a constant reminder that life is meant to be lived. Dance with Death, won't you?

—Rosita

Death Is not the Enemy...

If you ever want to witness first-hand an event where there is usually standing room only, loved ones dressed to the nines, and a lot of positive accolades delivered so emotionally and passionately to the *guest of honour,* drop by your local funeral home; after all, the guest of honor will be you some day.

Treated like royalty in most cases, you will lie peacefully in an expensive box while mourners come before you to say a final prayer, pay final respect; and, let's face it, some come out of sheer curiosity and/or to get final verification that you are indeed dead. For those of us with the really busy schedules, who are unable to attend, throw your guilt to the wind, because I understand that we can now boast about the development of drive-through visitations. Yes, you heard me right! Just drive right up and view your dead loved one (or not), and then off to your next meeting, or point of destination. Lord knows, you don't want to be late, or miss those important deadlines (no pun intended).

Frankly, funerals churn my stomach, because I don't like looking at dead bodies, loved ones or not. Nor will I allow mine to be on display when I've danced my final dance of life. My first pet peeve about funerals and death, is the fact that what should have been said to our loved ones while they were still alive and able to appreciate it, is usually said when the recipient is dead. That makes absolutely no sense to me. Imagine the kind of world we'd live in if we really said these kind words and acknowledgements to people while they were alive. I've always wondered what it would be like to have my funeral before I died... well that's for another book altogether.

My second pet peeve is the bad rap that death has been given. She has been described as a powerful force not to be reckoned with, a raging storm without a cause, and the very mention of her name is equated with evil, doom and gloom, and unfairness. Oh, how they've misjudged her.

Contrary to popular belief, she doesn't suddenly appear on any given day, or at any given moment, and snatch away our lives or the lives of those we love; she is not the Wicked Witch of the West. This is not how she orchestrates her moves.

Ironically, She is in love with life, and we are life; she wants to be a part of our lives until there is no more life. Did you know that Death lives in each and every one of us, and that we are death just as surely as we are life? **Stop!** Listen, and feel her presence at this very moment. She is beckoning you to the dance floor of life! If you cannot see Death or feel Death at this very moment in all her wisdom, and if you cannot silence all the demons that send unfounded and toxic messages about who she really is, then you will never truly experience the true meaning of life, and all its ecstasy.

Do not fear the very essence of life itself. Death is not a dark cloud hovering above us, seductively planning how to bring our lives to an end. She is instead a constant reminder that life is meant to be lived. Death is our teacher, our mentor, our constant reminder that nothing lasts forever, and that we must treasure every second of the day and live it completely and joyfully.

Find time today, and every day, to dance with the ones you love; talk with them, walk with them, say "I love you" a thousand times a day; celebrate life with them, bring them flowers or small tokens of your appreciation, sing with them, let them know they are important to you. Find every reason under the sun to celebrate who they are and your relationship with them, and then you will have lived life to the fullest with the ones you hold near and dear to your heart.

The greatest joy we could ever possibly find when the inevitable death lays our loved ones down to rest, is knowing with our deepest convictions that we lived life with them to the absolute fullest, and that their loving and nurturing spirits will soar forever in our beating hearts. *Go now and embrace the ones you love before the final curtain call.*

True wisdom will never be found tucked away between the pages of a book, or from the teachings of others, but rather, true wisdom comes from knowing oneself completely.

—Rosita

Meet Your Wizards of Oz

Discovering and Utilizing the Gifts that Keep on Giving

Have you ever really journeyed down yonder to the "Land of the Authentic Self?" You know, the land where three extraordinary and critical elements to our existence and overall health and well-being dwell? Meet *heart, soul,* and *spirit.* I like to refer to them as our "Wizards of Oz." These precious God-given gems live inside each and every one of us; longing, and so desperately waiting, for us to bring their magic, music, and passion to life. This can only be done if we choose to journey within to the "Land of the Authentic Self." The trip itself will be the most critical and beneficial journey you will ever take in a lifetime. Why? Because we need to be aware of, connected to, and provide ongoing nutrition and care to our "Wizards of Oz."

A healthy relationship, and ongoing care and nurturing of our "Wizards of Oz" is crucial, because they are the keepers of the five most powerful gifts or resources that we need to support us on our journey of life. They are the materials we need, to build and maintain a foundation that is sturdy enough to brave any of our storms of life.

A strong foundation provides a haven as a place to go when we need to *refuel, regroup, soul search, find inner peace and deeper meaning*—a process that is necessary and basic to human growth and survival.

If you've never journeyed within and truly connected with heart, soul and spirit, then trust me, you really haven't begun to live and experience life to its fullest! You gotta go there … it's a trip worth every cent, emotionally, mentally, and spiritually. Word of caution—**beware**—getting there may not be as easy as you think. Like our family homes, if the internal self has been neglected, ignored or unattended to for an extended period of time, things become dusty, cluttered and a little unsettled. A little internal housekeeping may be in order before you can really appreciate the true value of the trip.

You see, our God-given gems were pure and orderly when they were first given to us, but like anything else, become tired and dilapidated if not given the proper nutritional care. We usually slack off in the internal housekeeping department because we are just too darn busy and stressed out. The irony of it all, is that this is where our greatest refueling system lies. We also slack off because we are just too afraid to get to know our real selves. Depending on our past, it can be emotionally draining. The reality, however, is that any internal trip being initiated and worth taking in our adult years, will always have an emotional price tag attached to it.

We have already had life experiences, both good and bad, that have shaped our attitudes and our belief systems. These experiences will affect the logistics of our trip. In some cases, the highway to the "Land of the Authentic Self " will be paved with layers of toxic wastes, such as guilt, fear, anxiety, despair, hurt, shame, grief, and so on, that have not been dealt with, and or have been dismissed. That's what happens when we get behind in our housework. Those toxic wastes can become roadblocks that must be acknowledged and dealt with, before we can truly utilize the gifts awaiting our arrival in the "Land of the Authentic Self."

This clearing of the highway is tough, and sometimes takes years to complete, depending on how long it has been left unattended. Neglected internal highways are dangerous, and can cause havoc, because in most cases, the precious gems, which we need on our journey called life, have been buried under a lot of garbage, leaving us *selfless*.

If that's the case, how does one surface through the layers of toxic energy and waste to meet their "Wizards of Oz" (heart, soul, and spirit), and embrace life's precious gifts that they hold?

We must come face-to-face with the man/woman in the mirror and understand who he/she is. We are a society scared to death of ourselves.

Can you remember how much as a child you loved mirrors, and that wonderful image you saw staring back at you? Do you remember how you were mesmerized by what you saw? When was the last time you spent some time in front of the mirror? I don't mean fixing your hair, putting on makeup, or trimming your moustache. I'm talking about a face-to-face reunion with that reflection in the mirror.

If it's been a while, or not at all, start the process now! Remember, the present moment is all we really have. Grab a mirror and ask yourself these four important questions:

1. **Do I really know this person in the mirror?**
2. **Am I who I say I am?**
3. **Do I live what I speak?**
4. **Is this all that I am about?**

I can almost guarantee you that you will need some time to answer these questions honestly. Any one of us could weasel through these four questions and simply answer "Yes, Yes, Yes, Yes!" But it's the truth, and only the truth will set you free emotionally, mentally, physically and spiritually.

You must employ positive self-talk on a daily basis. Even if you are not ready, "fake it 'til you make it!" When you arrive at the point where you truly believe what you are saying, the roadblocks will slowly disappear one by one, and the highway will become free for you to travel. Miracles will start to unfold as you gradually feel yourself journeying within. It all starts with the exercise of self-talk. Repeat these messages (you may want to choose ones that resonate most with you), and say them to yourself daily:

1. I am an awesome human being, because God doesn't make junk.

2. I will make mistakes and wrong choices, but that doesn't make me a worthless individual. I will not make the same mistakes over and over again. That's self-defeating behavior.

3. I must have the courage to forgive others, so that I may free myself. Hanging on to anger will eventually leave me powerless.

4. I know that no one can promise me a rose garden, so I shall plant my own garden of roses.

5. I know faith can see me through almost anything, if first I can truly believe that I am worth it.

6. I will not allow anyone to disturb my peace of mind.

7. I have control over my actions because now, as an adult, I can make my own choices.

8. I know that it is okay for me to express my feelings (happy, sad, angry), as long as I do it in a way that is appropriate and non-threatening to others. It is okay, and it is normal to have these feelings, as long as I don't hold onto any particular one in a way that will entrap me and keep me from moving forward in a positive direction.

9. I am proud of who I am with all of my flaws. I will strive for excellence, not perfection.

10. I must always forgive myself and care for myself first.

11. I am not perfect, and yet I am still special.

12. Contentment and internal peace come from living in the present moment. Living in the past imprisons me. The future holds no guarantees. **Now** is all that I truly have. The magic is in the present moment!

When we employ self-talk, and truly believe and live what we are saying; when we are able to really understand, respect, and love all of who we are; if we are willing to change those parts we don't like, or that don't fit us anymore, then, and only then, can we start the process of freeing ourselves!

The *heart* light comes on, the *soul* comes to life again, and the *spirit* will rise up to meet every situation along life's journey, because it is then that your "Wizards of Oz" will reveal to you the most precious commodities, the greatest gifts life has to offer: *Self-love, self-esteem, self-respect, self-forgiveness, and self-care.* Without them, you are nothing! With them, you are a walking powerhouse, ready to travel any road you choose. You become courageous enough to overcome any obstacles that stand before you; opportunities now become boundless.

The journey within is indeed a personal investment. As a result of taking the trip, you become more focused, more relaxed, more grounded, and more aware of your boundless potential and the opportunities available to you. Your demons and inner critics become weakened, and forced to take a back seat. You begin to understand that you are more then just intellectual beings and that you also have many creative and spiritual facets upon which you can draw from for strength and guidance.

In our day-to-day struggles, we have a tendency to forget that we are multidimensional. We use such a large percentage of our brain power intellectualizing, and solving the mysteries of life, technology, politics and whatever else we can squeeze in; neglecting other critical aspects of ourselves. So our quest, then, is to ensure a balance between our *intellectual, spiritual,* and *creative* selves.Stay in touch with, and be aware at all times of the state of your *heart, soul,* and *spirit,* because they are the keepers of your precious gifts. In times of uncertainty, upheaval, change, balancing family and work, and our ongoing search for a deeper meaning of life, we should be true to ourselves by journeying to the "Land of the Authentic Self" regularly. In doing this, we can rejuvenate, utilize our reserves, remember who we are at any point in our lives, and be assured our abilities, talents and unlimited resources will always have a firm foundation on which to stand, when we have to come face-to-face with the "big bad wolves" of life.

It is only when we choose to accept who we are, with all of our strengths and our weaknesses, or when we choose to change those parts about ourselves that we feel uncomfortable with, that we will be able to truly love ourselves and others.

—Rosita

Keeping Heart, Soul, and Spirit Alive

What's Love Got to Do with It?

A line in a song by singer/songwriter George Benson, called the "Greatest Love of All," says: **"learning to love your-self is the greatest love of all."** Self-love is an omnipotent resource. It prepares us for a lifetime of loving and nurturing relationships. When we become grounded in self-love, it allows us to experience and participate in the most electrifying and powerful exchange of energy between human beings: the exchange of unconditional love. So, what is unconditional love? If you are so inclined, please turn to 1 Corinthians 13, verses 4-8, and you will have your answer.

> *Love is patient, love is kind. It does not envy,*
> *It does not boast, it is not proud. It is not rude,*
> *it is not self-seeking, it is not easily angered, it keeps no record*
> *of wrongs. Love does not delight in evil but rejoices with the*
> *truth. It always protects, always trusts, always hopes, always*
> *perseveres. Love never fails.*

This magnificent and godly exchange of energy is something every human being deserves to experience in full blossom. So, where do we begin to ensure the likelihood of this happening, so that we become a society of loving souls?

This process needs to begin in our childhood, and requires ongoing nurturance into, and throughout, our adult years. The ability to love ourselves and others unconditionally is necessary for basic survival, because it brings our heart, soul, and spirit to life!

As parents/guardians, it is our responsibility to be role models, and to leave a loving and lasting legacy for our children about how to love themselves and others. Who among us would not want their children to feel loved, be touched by love, and to give love in a caring and passionate way that fuels their "Wizards of Oz," and engages them in a lifetime of strong, healthy, and nurturing relationships? To increase the likelihood of this occurring, children need to be a part of a life with, and model the behavior of, loving and esteemed parents/guardians. It is through this type of bonding, as well as the relationships developed with other influential adults in their lives, that children learn to feel *valued, loved, acknowledged, appreciated, respected, and esteemed*; all of which fuels self-love. If children do not have a firm foundation of self-love and self-respect, the odds of maintaining loving and healthy relationships into their adult years is next to nil. It is within our power to model and teach our children, and generations to follow, how to foster a foundation for establishing healthy, loving relationships.

Are you prepared to participate in this process? Do you have what it takes to be a teacher for our future generations? Will you be able to leave a legacy of loving relationships? Do you love yourself unconditionally? Can you show others how to love in a safe, nurturing, and caring way? Walk yourself through these five simple steps below, and see how ready you are to participate in the process. If we are to be loving and esteemed role models, then we need to have a firm foundation in relation to the five steps listed below:

Step 1: Are you grounded in self-love?

Re-evaluate how you've come to understand, express, and experience love by reviewing, and honestly answering the questions below:

Who taught you about giving and receiving love, and what was that experience like for you? Did you feel loved as a child, and do you now, as an adult? If so, do you nurture this love on an ongoing basis? Did you have, and do you continue to have, loving and caring role models in your life?

Do you feel that you have a firm foundation of self-love and self-

respect? Would you consider yourself a person with high self-esteem? Do you care passionately for yourself? Do you practice self-discipline, self-forgiveness, and self-acceptance?

Do you feel good about how you love, and how it is reciprocated?

Step 2: When was the last time you had a reunion or a first time meeting with that reflection staring back at you in the mirror?

This is very important because I believe that the key to self-love is self-discovery. We learn to love ourselves by learning about ourselves and accepting ourselves for who we really are. This is a process that should be initiated in our childhood; if it is not, then as adults we must take the journey, and discover the truths about ourselves. Re-visit the self-awareness exercises in the previous chapter.

Step 3: Are you a 'stinkin' thinker or a positive thinker?

What do you think about all day? We become what we think. All the words we say, as well as our actions, are self-defining statements. They say, "This is who I am." Do you need to release yourself from negative and self-defeating thoughts and behaviors?

We need to have positive self-regard if we are to love ourselves, others, and to teach our children about love. You are fine because God doesn't make junk! When the negative chatter and behaviors surface, say this quietly to yourself: "I am much bigger than that thought or action." Quickly think of some positive thoughts, dreams, affirmations, and possibilities. If you can change your thoughts, you can change your world.

Step 4: Are you living in the magic of the moment?

You are a beautiful and awesomely equipped individual, worthy of love and healthy, loving relationships. Simply choose not to be a prisoner, and let go of those things/thoughts that keep you in emotional and mental turmoil. This prevents love from radiating. As an adult, you are now the decision maker. Let the past be exactly that, the past. Move forward with the type of thinking that takes you into the present moment, and then moves you off into the future. You are now in charge of your life, and your thoughts.

Step 5: Do you care for and nurture yourself emotionally, mentally, spiritually, and physically?

An important aspect of self-love is self-nurturance. Self-care ignites personal affection and self-esteem. When we care for ourselves we feel better about ourselves and our relationships with others. Engage in and continually practice self-care techniques on a daily basis.

When we truly love and respect ourselves, self-care becomes as basic as brushing our teeth every day. It becomes an essential part of our daily routine.

How did you do? Take some time to digest your answers; write them down on a piece of paper if you need to. The purpose of this exercise is to allow you to come to an understanding about how grounded you are in self-love, your level of self-confidence, your self-esteem, and whether or not you feel loved enough to support another human being on his/her journey toward self-love.

A happy and healthy relationship with yourself radiates love, passion and energy. That energy can spread like wildfire and can touch many lives.

Each and every one of us was brought into this world to be a part of this magical bliss which keeps us grounded, connected, and alive as human beings. It is a wonderful awakening! If you come to the conclusion that you have what it takes to support another human being through this process, then congratulations; you now have an important role to play in ensuring that we become a society of loving souls! If not, don't give up, stay true to yourself, and understand that you are worth loving, and sharing that love with others. Continue going over the necessary steps as outlined, until you feel ready to start on the path towards self-love and loving relationships.

There are many types of loving relationships in which we can engage, such as those between a husband and a wife, friends, siblings, a parent and child and so on. What you must understand, is that they are all ignited and maintained by the same common fuel: self-love. The presence of self-love allows us to approach each of these relationships differently but in an honorable and respectful way. It also allows us to clearly communicate what our expectations are when we willingly engage in loving relationships.

Our constant bombardment of 'love gone wrong' songs; our daily doses of soap opera television, which, in most cases, depicts a line from one of Tina Turner's greatest hits, "What's love got to do with it?"; and our drive-through approach to loving and healthy relationships, can become confusing, scary, and yes, a little crazy, too. That is why we must be well-grounded in our views about love, establish our boundaries, and understand who we are, and what we have to give, in relation to love and loving relationships.

I've witnessed what was supposedly loving relationships in my family, between friends, co-workers, and with many of my clients over the past twenty years as a social worker. The common denominator that destroyed these relationships was that self-love was missing. That powerful God-given exchange of energy couldn't unveil itself. These relationships were formed with one or both people lacking self-respect, self-esteem, self-control, self-worth, and self-affection, all of which are critical to establishing healthy, loving relationships. Such relationships are often built with the expectation of fulfilling an unmet childhood need for love, or attempting to feed an emotionally starved ego lacking spiritual basis, or is oftentimes built on a general misconception about what an unconditional loving relationship is all about.

In these types of relationships, love cannot be magnified in a beautiful and radiant way. As a result, unhealthy and destructive physical, emotional, and mental behavior presents itself, and is often rationalized with a phrase such as, "well, you know that I still love you." You and I know that love is not supposed to *offend* or *abuse* in any way; not physically, emotionally, mentally, spiritually or financially. If it does, then it is clearly not love. Love is not selfless, and this type of behavior screams out: "I am selfless, and I don't know how to love you or myself!"

Giving and receiving love go hand-in-hand. If we can't experience the joy of giving love, chances are we won't be able to receive it. The people you surround yourself with and give your love to, must clearly see that love is a two-way street. Love doesn't survive and cannot radiate itself in all its wonder if it travels down a one-way street. For those of us who journey on the two-way street of love, we know what it's like when love shines so brightly, and we know that sharing and receiving this magical energy is the ultimate ecstasy. It is an absolute adrenaline rush. Love does indeed make the world go round, and it is indeed a universal language. Love gives us the ability to communicate with absolutely anyone because it can be communicated through a simple smile, an expression, a touch, or an act of kindness. "What's love got to do with it?" Absolutely everything!

Refuse to be seduced by the materialistic serpents in life who try desperately to convince you and me that money is the only source which leads to true happiness. If you want to find true happiness, start by focusing on and appreciating the small blessings that surround us each and every day.

—*Rosita*

Listen to the Children and Live in the Magic of the Moment

When was the last time you slowed down the pace long enough to experience calm, serenity, silence, nature's bliss, a song in your heart, a dance with your child, a special time with your spouse? (The list goes on and on). Has it been too long? Unfortunately, many of us reach out in desperation for such important moments when we are forced to, such as when we are experiencing a sudden sickness or loss. Don't wait for that to happen before you engage in these types of deserving experiences. I encourage you to start right now by embracing every tender moment that life presents to you, and then savouring it, because this life is the *real thing,* and you can never replay those special moments again.

Let me share by way of an example, where I am coming from. One morning as I was coming out of the shower with a towel wrapped around me, and a zillion thoughts in my head, my son Joshua, who was eight years old at the time, knocked on the door and asked if he could come in because he had something he wanted me to see. I told him I was getting dressed and asked if it could wait. He said yes, but returned again shortly (I'm sure to him a lot of time had passed since his knock), and before I could say a word he burst into the room and rambled on about what a great job he had done cleaning up his room and how I just had to see how it looked; he was totally oblivious to the fact that I was still getting dressed. In bewilderment I said, "But Josh, can't you see I am still getting dressed? Give Mom some privacy. I need to finish putting my clothes on."

At that point, the look on his face said it all. *The moment was lost*; the excitement had diminished; the thrill was over. In his mind, I would probably never make it to his room to see his fine efforts.

As he walked slowly from the room, he closed the door and I could hear him saying, "This wouldn't even matter if Adam and Eve hadn't eaten the forbidden fruit." I couldn't believe what I was hearing, so I opened the door and said, "What did you say?" He repeated it again, except this time he added, "If they hadn't done that, Mom, then you would have come to see my room because it wouldn't have mattered if you were dressed or not." So there I was, guilty as charged, for not living in the "magic of the moment." My mind was focused on other 'stuff,' and not sharing in Joshua's joyous occasion. I didn't truly understand how important it was to him until he made that statement. It took me all of five seconds to throw on a bathrobe, go into his room and see the terrific job he had done.

Joshua reminded me about how important the "magic of the moment" really is, and how we need to live life, and experience life, in each and every moment of our lives. That's where the magic lies. Outside of that, what really matters?

We must not fall prey, as Adam and Eve did, to the tempting and mouth-watering traps set by the crafty serpents in life, who try seductively to convince us that there is other 'stuff' in life far more important than sharing in the magic of the moment. We must be careful not to spend too much of our time on those things in life that really don't mean a lot in the greater scheme of things. Be present in all aspects of life with those you hold near and dear to your heart. If you truly want to understand this concept better, and experience present-moment living, what really matters, and what life is all about, spend a day with a child in his world. See the beauty, the innocence, and sincerity through their eyes. Let them be your role model. All that they experience is what is going on at that moment.

My youngest son, Christian, who was five at the time, taught me yet another lesson about being alive and alert for the present moment. During dinnertime, whenever it was his turn to bless the food, I could feel myself getting restless, cranky, and hungry, because his prayers could be quite lengthy. Meanwhile my stomach would be doing back flips, saying "feed me." But one night I decided that, in fairness to Christian, I would really give him my undivided attention, and that's exactly what I did, because prior to that, all I was focusing on was when he would be finished so I could eat. So I listened intently as Christian prayed one night, "Dear God, thank you for the walls, for the ceiling, for the roof, for my mom's eyes, for the floors, for the table....," and the prayer went on and on. When he finished, I didn't feel that hungry anymore, because my heart had been touched, and filled with inspiration, and so I thanked him for such a nice prayer.

You see, once again it took a child to remind me of the power of capturing and staying in the present moment, and the important blessings I had around me, which I had been taking for granted— things like a roof over my head, because at that moment there were, and still are, people sleeping in the streets; for my eyes, because at that moment many were and continue to be blind; for the table that was filled with food and love, because at that moment many people starving in the world would have gladly traded places with me.

Since that day, I listen to Christian's messages, and I am constantly reminded about how blessed I truly am. I am now able to recognize small blessings that I have, that many may never come to truly appreciate, because they are blinded by the 'stuff' in life.

One of my greatest motivators in life is knowing that no matter what I accumulate in terms of money or material things here on earth, nothing will compare to what my children have given me, and what I can and will leave for my children by way of example: emotionally, mentally, and spiritually; and the irony of it all is that the saying "what comes around, goes around," is so true, because I've learned it all from them. It is simply this: Love a lot, laugh a lot, sing a lot, dance a lot, play fair, play safe, keep the heart light turned on, go to the edge, and never ever let anyone tell you that you are not good enough, or allow anyone to "pooh pooh" on your dreams. You can be all that you want to be. Life is yours for the taking! Don't let that pollutant 'stuff' get in your way. Take every moment that life serves up to you and say, "Come on life, I'm ready to live!" and then do just that. Tomorrow may be too late!

Once I was able to conceptualize my being human, and that it was okay to do what felt right to me at any given moment, I truly started living.

—*Rosita*

Good for Me!

A Creed to Live By

When I am feeling confused or upset and I come to you for support and you listen to me, I say, **"good for me,"** for having the courage to come to you.

When I need some *me* time and I recognize this, and I quietly go into myself, I say, **"good for me,"** for realizing that I am human.

When I come home at the end of the day and I'm exhausted and I don't feel like making supper and I push speed dial to the nearest Pizza Hut, I say, **"good for me,"** for realizing that I can't do it all and that mothers are people too.

When I close a chapter on a relationship that's not healthy for me I say, **"good for me,"** for finding the strength and the courage to take good care of myself.

When I am able to forgive others, I say, **"good for me"** for setting myself free emotionally, spiritually, and physically.

When I make a mistake or screw up royally, I say, **"good for me,"** for not needing to be perfect.

When I'm feeling physically, emotionally, mentally, or spiritually fatigued, and I hide under the covers for a day, I say, **"good for me,"** for giving myself permission to escape from my responsibilities for a day.

When I'm having a blah type of day and I need a pick-me-up, and I go for my "retail therapy" and buy that dress I can't afford, I say, **"good for me,"** for having the sense to use my husband's credit card.

When someone asks me for a favor and I have to say no, I say, "good for me," for recognizing that it is OK to say no.

When I give myself permission to swing in the park, play in the sand, roll down a hill, play on the monkey bars, and own a toy or two, I say, "good for me," for never losing the spirit of the child within me.

When Saturday rolls around and I feel like eating bonbons and lazing in my pajamas all day, and I ignore the door bell and my phone messages, I say, "good for me," for having the sense to know that just because the phone rings and the door bell sounds, it doesn't mean I have to answer them.

When I turn up the stereo and dance around the house in hysterics, I say, "good for me," for not needing any drugs to get my kicks!

When I spend endless time with my husband and children, and we play, dance, laugh, and have "mega fun" together, I say, "good for me," for being blessed with three of the most interesting and lovable guys I know.

And at the end of the day when I lie down to rest, and I think about my day, and I replay it over and over again because I did what I wanted to do, I say, "good for me," for being in control of my day and for not wanting to erase any of it.

And when I dream what some may call the impossible dream, and see my victory at the end of it all, I say, "good for me," for having the courage to dream.

And because I will never say "never," and I will always dream, and I will not be the person who says, "if I had my life to live over again," I say "good for me," for seizing every moment of every day and truly loving life, because I'm worth it....

There is no greater wealth to hold onto than your health. Listen to the wisdom of your body; it speaks to each of us in volumes. Pay attention to the "caution, proceed slowly" signs.

—*Rosita*

Can't Catch Me!

I'll run and run as fast as I can. You can't catch me.
I'm the Gingerbread Man!

Unfortunately, this childhood tale doesn't have a happy ending. Recall that the Gingerbread Man is eaten alive by the Sly Old Fox. Today, many of us live our lives like the Gingerbread Man, running relentlessly from our self-imposed responsibilities, and the day-to-day pressures, hoping that they don't catch up to us.

It is no secret that we are over-extended emotionally, mentally, physically, and financially, and that we have forgotten how to slow down. We've lost the art of sleeping, which is a natural restorative process. We've forgotten how to laugh, relax, play, and love unconditionally.

In our desperate search for a blissful life, we destroy the very essence of life itself. We knowingly and unknowingly sacrifice the *self,* our very own existence, to a fast-paced lifestyle that makes us *fair game* for the Sly Old Fox, which in our case, is sickness and disease. We are convinced that the harder we run and the faster we go, the better off we'll be. We continue the race operating in *overdrive,* running all the red lights and ignoring the "caution, proceed slowly" signs, until one day it all catches up to us, and we crash. We feel helpless, lifeless, and defeated.

Like the Gingerbread man, we've been "baked," "fried," or as some of us call it, "burnt out!" We have reached the pinnacle of *self-* imposed destruction. Are we suicidal, or what? Why weren't we listening to the wisdom of our bodies? Remember those sniffles, headaches, panic attacks, mood swings, and feelings of anxiety, anger, and the inability to sleep? That was your body speaking so loudly.

You see, we cannot fool the body, nor can we constantly abuse it without some repercussions. The body keeps score, and constantly sends out signals and reminders to us to *slow down, take some time to relax, and get some perspective.* Yet, our response is always the same: "as soon as I finish this final report," or, "I'll start tomorrow." Thus, the journey down the road of broken promises to the *self* begins.

Our bodies will crash if we continue to deprive them of tender love and care. You are hereby *being given notice that unless you start taking care of yourself, you are going to die a lot sooner than you think.* We all know that Death has the final say in this dance of life, but what's with the personal invitation for her to come sooner? Let Death come in her own sweet time.

Many of us are not comfortable giving ourselves permission to take down time, and engaging in activities of self-care and nurturance that really bring our hearts and souls to life. We often feel that we are copping out if we take a break; don't forget: the "harder we run, the better off we'll be" theory! How sad it is to know that many of us are still of that mindset.

So how do we slow ourselves down? How do we get ourselves out of the *Gingerbread Man mode*? Well, it's really not that difficult. First, I would suggest that we need to make a commitment to a lifestyle change, by choosing to live a balanced life, which means balancing our time between those things that we have to do, with those things we choose to do, and finding time for personal self-care.

Secondly, it means releasing the internal "mute" button that keeps us trapped in unhealthy behavioral patterns, and starting to turn up the volume on our hearts, souls, and physical selves so that we can listen attentively to the wisdom of our bodies, and live a truly dynamic and healthy lifestyle.

The third suggestion would be to shut down and go home, emotionally, mentally, and physically. We need to *stop, look* and *lis-*

ten to ourselves. It really is okay to do that. It doesn't make us any less human beings. So, shut down the computer, leave the briefcase at work, turn off the cell phones and pagers, turn off the television, and tune in to that special you. If you need further convincing, imagine that someone has video-recorded your activities for the entire day without you being aware of it. Would you want it played back, and if you did, what would your reaction be?

As a point of clarification, I don't want you to think that I don't recognize the value and importance of work, because for most of us it's a necessary means so that we can eat and sleep and with a roof over our heads. For some, it's a form of personal validation; and the list goes on.

What I am trying to communicate here, is that while work is important, it shouldn't occupy our every thought. It should be a very small component compared to the other things in life that really matter. This applies even if we truly enjoy our jobs. We are more than just our job descriptions. Finally, we have to stop making excuses for our fast pace, and for not taking care of ourselves. We have to stop using such worn-out excuses as a lack of time, or other phrases such as, *"I'm doing it to make a better life for my children"; "It's so busy I can't take time off."* My favorite one is: *"I'm working this hard so that I'll have enough money to retire."* At this frantic pace, the only retirement you'll see is one that leads directly to a comfy bed in a pine box, surrounded by flowers you'll never smell; and you will definitely be retired for good. That can't possibly be your idea of a comfortable retirement, or is it? Holding on to our bag of excuses will only keep us stagnated and unhealthy!

Practising the art of self-care is a critical ingredient in life, because it reminds us how important we are, and to be good to ourselves. It reminds us that if we don't become selfish, we become selfless. *Your health is your wealth!*

My true obsession with self-care and spiritual renewal came from my experiences as a social worker, and from watching my colleagues in the helping profession giving to others while sacrificing the *self.* I found it heart-wrenching to see professionals, mostly women, so caught up in their need to help others and to get the job done, that there was no *me* time in their day-to-day activities. They were silently killing themselves. Sadder still is the fact that they didn't realize what they were doing to themselves, until, as happened in a few cases, it was too late. *Death accepted their invitation.* Trust me, this is one invitation you can't retract.

My colleagues were passionate about supporting those in need, but lost the passion for themselves. Simply put, some of them were unable to separate themselves from work. Late one fall afternoon, in 1999, as I sat on the stairs outside of my former workplace waiting for a ride home, a gentleman, who was approximately seventy years old, was passing by; he smiled and then asked, "All finished for the day?" To which I replied "Yep." He then said, "I thought so, because you look so relaxed, and that's good, because you have to save some of your energy for when you get to be my age." I didn't think much of it at the time, but a few hours later it hit me like a ton of bricks: "Save some of your energy for when you get to be my age." What a powerful statement, and what great words of advice from a total stranger. They are now words that I live by each and every day. I've slowed down the pace, I relax more, and I don't have this compulsive need to be busy or feel guilty if I'm not. I want to have *energy and my health* for when I get to be the age of that kind gentleman.

I thank my angels for the wonderful opportunity to have met this kind and wise man who has had a distinct impact on my life, and who added to my awareness of the importance of self-care. What a blessing! I hope you, too, will carry his message with you, always!

The body is an incredible gift from God. Only He could create such a wonder. I show my unwavering gratitude to Him every day by choosing to take care of mine.

—*Rosita*

Me First!! (for a change)

Being true to yourself by taking care of yourself, first, is not selfish. If you get tricked into believing that it is, or that you're not worthy of it, you will become selfless.

—*Rosita*

Self-care has played a major role in my life, from grade school right through to my adult life. The physical, emotional, and mental strength that I reap from taking care of myself is what keeps me passionately connected to it. Eventually, I followed up on that enjoyment, became involved in fitness clubs, and became certified as a fitness consultant. I taught aerobic classes for about seven years on a part-time basis, while I continued my full-time job as a social worker.

My desire to teach fitness classes came as the result of watching my peers stand next to me in my fitness classes struggling to do yet one more push-up, or two more minutes of aerobics. I so desperately wanted to yell, over "come on, you can do it!"

Teaching fitness classes was, and probably still is, one of the most rewarding experiences I have ever had. To this day, I am still amazed at how I could convince a woman that, yes, she could do two more push-ups, or two more minutes of aerobics, if she put her mind to it. When she did, she was always able to do what she thought was the impossible. My slogan was: "The mind can move the body."

Once my participants believed this, it was amazing what they were able to accomplish on a physical basis. It was so cool watching them make the body and mind connection: *if the head said yes to a reasonable request, the body could follow through.* My overall message was: "whatever you believe can be achieved."

My passion about the issues relating to self-care from both a physical and mental perspective, was a natural transition to my next journey in life; and has, again, given me the opportunity to touch many lives and develop interesting and fun relationships.

During the past five years, I have traveled through North America and the United States as a Professional Speaker. What a revelation and an awesome experience! The majority of my speaking contracts have been with organizations in the workplace. In most cases, I am being hired to breathe new life into the employees through a message of inspiration, motivation, and humour.

The issues that organizations are dealing with in most instances, are developing techniques to keep their employees motivated. They often ask, "How do I get them to buy into the fact that this is our company/organization?"; "How do we mend broken spirits affected by change, change, change, and constant upheaval in the workplace?"

Having led an organization through some of the same temporary setbacks in the role of Executive Director, I am now thrilled to go into workplaces and ignite energy levels and shaky spirits again! Words can't explain the adrenaline rush that comes with supporting people on their journey to new heights. It's an incredible experience.

To walk into a room of one hundred-plus people and to walk out an hour later knowing that I may have saved a starving soul, touched a battered heart, re-awakened someone's dreams, or pushed them all to a new level of discovery, is the greatest gift a speaker could ever hope to receive—and the message I deliver is really quite simple: "Care for yourself passionately, and everything else will fall into place."

Managing any kind of change, adversity or upheaval in our workplace or on a personal level requires the management of "self" first. What I have observed in my work with companies/organizations is that those folks who were caring for themselves in a passionate way (physically, emotionally, mentally and spiritually), incorporated fun into their lives on and off the job, and understood that they were more than just their job descriptions.

They weathered the storms noticeably better than those who did not adhere to the *me first!* philosophy. They were also in touch with, and were utilizing, their internal resources.

The next few pages will provide you with some fun information which I present to my audiences to help them stay connected to self care, fun, and change in both their personal and work lives. I hope that you will benefit from some of the material as you begin, or continue to incorporate, self-care into your daily living.

Step 1

Hello, and welcome to the neighborhood of self-care. Your garbage day is today. Are you going to set yours out for disposal? Self-care begins with letting go of those negative thoughts (garbage) and tired excuses that occupy our time and keep us from doing good things for ourselves. Remember, time is of the essence.

We all know that if we leave our garbage sitting around too long it can start to stink in a big way! Put away the recycling bin, because when we are dealing with the human mind, heart, and soul, nothing is recyclable. All toxic waste products must be disposed of forever! Look deep inside your heart and soul—what do you want to dispose of?

Having trouble deciding what to get rid of? Let me be of assistance.

Item #1: Get rid of all of your "Somebody's done me wrong" songs.

Okay, so you've had a bad day, or maybe even a bad week; perhaps a bad month or, even worse, just maybe you've had a bad life, a life that you feel you were not deserving of. If this is true, then where do you go from here? The answer is simple—

pick yourself up, dust yourself off, and show life what you're truly made of, instead of coming unglued or blaming everyone every time you hit a bump in life; an unexpected turn, or some other misfortune.

Don't fall back into the "Life's not fair; somebody's done me wrong" tune! Instead, we should all look for the lesson in our experiences, do some self-reflecting, and see how we can turn the situation into something more positive. Hang onto faith, because sometimes that's all you will have to hang onto. All the darkness in the world cannot put out the light of a single candle.

Blaming others uses a lot of energy and places a damper on our faith. When we start losing energy and faith, we become vulnerable, tired, diseased, and cranky. Now there's a self-induced prescription for a 'living hell'. Re-focus that energy on making your situation better, and move forward!

Item #2: Lose the "Achy Breaky Heart" stories.

Who doesn't have an achy, breaky heart story lingering somewhere in their past? You know the one heartbreak story that keeps popping up just when you think you've tamed it or disposed of it. Life happens that way sometimes. We must not become so consumed with our past that it interferes with our present-moment living. If you live on planet Earth, and you haven't had your heart broken, experienced disappointments, missed opportunities, had a romance or friendship gone sour, or if you haven't been on the emotional roller coaster ride a few times over, or been treated unjustly, you must be either from another planet or you have mastered the art of escaping reality.

"Achy Breaky Heart" stories can smother us and place a tremendous burden on those people who have to listen to them. People will begin to tune you out, and eventually turn you off if you continually burden them with heartbreak stories. Acknowledge the heartache and pain in your life, learn the lesson, and embrace the present moment. This is necessary so that you can bring closure to the matter. As long as one painful door is left open, it is difficult to open a healthier one. If you can do that, you can then move in a positive direction towards daily self-care.

Item #3: Lose the "If only there were 48 hours in the day" fantasy.

Folks, it's reality check time! Listen carefully. The good Lord has given us twenty-four (count 'em) hours in a day. That's it. No matter how you do the math, you will never get any more than that. By the way, time does not stand still. Time is a one-way trip, and the sooner we digest that reality, the better off we will all be.

How many times have we heard people say, "There are simply not enough hours in a day," or "If I could turn back the hands of time," or "time wasn't on my side," and of course, my favorite, "I was hoping to find more time." Now where exactly were these people looking, and did they really expect to find more time? If the answer is yes, then I really hope they are under a physician's care.

We cannot control the pace at which time moves, nor can we bring it to a complete halt at any given time, but we can control how we manage our time in respect to our day-to-day activities. So let's get off the, "If only there were 48 hours in a day" fantasy bus. Let's plant our feet firmly on the ground, and start organizing our day according to the time that we know is available to us in the real world!

We spend large portions of our hard-earned money on fancy organizers, daytimers, calendars, etc. and still we can't seem to get our heads around time management. That's because there is still that little inner critic that tells us, "If only I had more time, everything would be all right." You must short circuit that little critter, and put him out of his misery for good; otherwise he will destroy you.

We all need to become *clock-wise*. Notice that the hands on the clock move in a forward direction, and not back. It is up to us to fill those seconds, minutes, and hours with *quality* so that at the end of the day we can feel a sense of accomplishment, are able to incorporate time for ourselves and our loved ones, and feel less guilt and anxiety.

Item #4: Lose the excuses, such as: "I'm tired"; "I don't have enough money or time"; "I'm scared"; or "I am married with children" (this is not Al Bundy Land).

Let me start by saying that excuses are a great way to ensure that we accomplish nothing, and have a meaningless life. Excuses strangle us emotionally and mentally, and disengage us from our awesome internal resources. The art of self-care includes making time for ourselves, nurturing our dreams, and being all that we were meant to be.

Please don't short-change yourself by contemplating a list of all the reasons why you can't experience life your way. We all get scared, anxious, and overwhelmed at the thought of trying new ideas, a different focus, or a new path, but please don't let these feelings stagnate you. Often, these excuses come out in a different format, and we may identify them with: "I am too tired"; "I'm too busy with the children"; "I'm married, and I have a lot of financial responsibilities," etc. Fear can entrap us. Take the leap and amazing things will happen.

An exercise I like to do with audiences when I am delivering a session on self-care is to ask them to write down one reality-based dream (a romantic night with Ricky Martin doesn't cut it) that they can, and want, to bring to fruition. Then I ask them to write down why the dream has not yet come to life. Once they've done that, I collect them all and then I pull out my Official Excuses Bag. I place all the dreams in this bag, and explain that I have thousands of dreams that lie dormant in bags like this on my bookshelf in my office, and many I know will never see the light of day! The impact of doing this exercise is powerful. I can suddenly see the audience sit up and take notice. In fact, I've had participants march up to the front of the room during my presentation, or during a break, and ask for their dreams back. You see, many of our dreams can come true, but we use excuse-making as a roadblock so that we don't have to go to the edge and make it happen. It's tough coming out of the "comfort zone." Living our dreams is part of the self-care exposition. If we want to display our wholeness, and appreciate and live life to the fullest, then this is a critical element that cannot be placed on the back burner. **Go for it!**

Remember, you have to start somewhere. Even if you are only able to toss one item at a time, that's ok. The important point is that you start the process now. Good luck!

Me First!! (for a change)

The Art of Self-Care

To become a champion of emotional, mental, physical, and spiritual self-care you must:

❑ **Laugh!** Laughing is indeed an art, and you are the artist. Why not paint laugh lines around your heart, soul, and spiritual well-being? When was the last time you had a deep-down-from-the-belly laugh, one that brought tears to your eyes and left you wondering if you would make it to the bathroom on time? Now that's laughing. Done that lately? It's no secret that laughter is the simplest and oldest prescription for all of life's unexpected woes. It is the best form of medicine. To me, it's that nutritional supplement we dropped from our diets ages ago because we got caught up in the fast-paced game called life ,which afforded us no time for laughter. I can guarantee you that if you start laughing, and stop taking yourself and life so seriously, you will do wonders for the ticker (heart).

❑ **Play, Play, Play!** There is no greater joy than watching children at play. They are uninhibited, take risks, laugh, scream, negotiate, trust, demonstrate their innocence; they tell each other exactly what they want, have superb imaginations, and simply remind us through their actions of the real meaning of life. If you don't own a toy, or have forgotten how to play with a special child in your life, doing child-like activities and bringing yourself into their world, then try it! Let the children take the lead. It's amazing what this will do for your spirit!

❑ **Fall deeply in love with yourself!** When was the last time you stood tall in the mirror with your head held high and announced "Oh, how I love me, let me count the ways"? My guess is that you haven't, and probably won't. Why? Because making such a statement in the eyes of many is *selfish* and *conceited*. Wrong! If we don't feel this way about ourselves, we become selfless. It is very difficult to give love unconditionally to others (no strings attached) if we don't first and foremost love ourselves in a big way. Now go ahead, get in front of a mirror, and let the party begin.

❑ **Become champions of faith. Embrace the mystery of what you don't know!** One of my favorite quotes says it all: "Come to the edge," he said, and they said, "But we are afraid," and he said "Come to the edge!" They came, he pushed them and they flew!" (*Guillaume Apollnaire*).

Post this quote in a place where you can stare at it every day, as a reminder that possibilities are endless, and that you have much to do and to experience, if you are ready for adventure and risks. Read it over and over again on any given day, when you are feeling unchallenged, unproductive, dealing with change, or challenged by the fear that keeps you from living the life you really want to live.

Flap those wings and go for it! When you do, your next quote will be this one: "And then the day came when the risk it took to remain tight in the bud became more painful then the risk it took to blossom" (*Anais Nin*). What a day that will be!

❑ **Surround yourself with "living people"; not the "living dead."** Have you ever been around, or been entertained by, certain people who always seem to have one foot in the grave and the other on a banana peel? Just one glance in their eyes will tell you that they live and breathe negativity. In fact, if you are around them for any length of time, you will begin to feel as though you are having the life sucked out of you. Toxic energy can choke your spirits. The *living dead* are dangerous people to be around. Quick, start your engine, and run as far away from these people as you can get!

❑ **Get turned on to yourself, so that people can get turned on to you!** "Mirror mirror on the wall who's the fairest of them all?" Grab a mirror right now and take a look at yourself. Is this a face that only a mother could love? You know the old saying: "A picture is worth a thousand words." Well, the one in the mirror is worth a million. The truth about what we are feeling and experiencing is written all over our faces. You can run, but you can't hide. How we look, and what we say, are reflections of who we are, and it's those signals that we send to others. Non-verbal information speaks volumes.

Getting turned on to yourself means setting time aside each day outside of your normal routines and steady pace, to devote some time to self-care, self-reflection, and solitude. How do people see you? How do you see yourself? Are you turning them on or off?

❑ **Unleash your skillful and creative talents!** What abundance we all have! Do not let it sit idle and under-utilized. Use your resources, recognize your worth, and be all that you can be, and then some!

❑ **Spend time with those you love!** The "drive-through" approach to love and relationships is making us wonder who is it that we truly love. In our mad rush out the door this morning was it our spouse or the mail man/woman we kissed good bye? Slow it down folks, demonstrate some real TLC. Take time to embrace those you love, look them deep in their eyes, tell them and show them that you love them so much. Love can't survive the drive-through approach. We are dealing with human hearts and emotions, not hamburgers and fries!

❑ **Develop personal goals and a personal mission statement.** If you do not know who you are or what you are about, don't expect others to, and don't expect to reach your highest potential. To be your personal best, and to journey in the right directions, you must first define who you are and what your expectations are in life.

❑ **Seek out professional development constantly. One can never stop learning.** A friend once said to me, "Once you get to a point in your life where you think you know everything, then you might as well be dead." She was right, because life is about growth and re-growth. When you're through learning, you're through!

❑ **Sleep!** It's a natural restorative process, yet millions of Canadians each night toss and turn, trying to figure out the best position to be in, so that they can get a good night's sleep and forget about the day's stresses. When that doesn't work, they reach for their bottle of sleep aids to help get them through yet another sleepless night. The body keeps score. We can't run on empty; the body will pay a price. Sleep allows the body to mend and refuel itself. Keep your bedroom off limits to the disgruntled boss, colleagues, friends, family members, clients, stress, and unfinished assignments etc. While it is inevitable that thoughts of work may occasionally sneak in at the supper table, or perhaps during a commercial break while you are relaxing watching television, please make a pact with yourself that it will never be welcomed in the bedroom. It takes time to emotionally do this, but it can happen, and it works. A half an hour or so before your bedtime, start thinking relaxing thoughts and doing relaxing activities, that will help you unwind and spend a peaceful night sleeping. To see if you are getting on track, each morning as you awake, ask yourself these three important questions: "Who did I sleep with last night?"; "Was it good?"; and "If it wasn't, what am I going to do about it?" Sleeping with work is like sleeping with the enemy!!

❑ **Eat!** Your health is your wealth, and if you are not putting good stuff in and eating a balanced diet, there will be a price to pay. Not only physically but emotionally, and mentally. Often when we are feeling cranky, tired and just simply fed up, it's because we are not eating properly. Food does have an impact on how we feel, and does affect our energy level.

❑ **Get physical:** The body was meant to be moved, so move it! Park your car and walk the twenty or thirty minutes to your next destination. Walking or any form of exercise releases stress and can take inches off the waist. It is recommended that any activity be done at least three times a week if you really want to achieve measurable results.

❑ **Celebrate!** When was the last time you kicked up your heels and had a "just because" celebration? Many of us leave the celebrations to birthdays, anniversaries, baptisms, births, and holidays. However, we should be celebrating each and every day. For me, I celebrate each day when I awaken for the many blessings, and abundance that God provides to me each day! Here's three cheers being sent your way for a day of *celebration* simply because you are you, and because you are alive.

❑ **Forgive!** Take a moment each day to forgive those who need to be forgiven. We need to do this because it allows us to *free up ourselves.* Holding on to the resentment, anger, and tales of somebody doing us wrong, just harbors heartache, heart disease, and ill health. Who needs that?

❑ **Dream!** Dream the impossible dream and live the possible. We are all made of dreams, both the possible and the impossible. However, priority needs to be given to the possible or reality-based dreams. Dreams give us our dose of *Chicken Soup for the Soul* and everybody needs a little more chicken soup. If we don't bring our dreams to life they quickly become *chicken poop for the soul,* and trust me, that's nothing to be proud of!

Try putting some of these tips into practice each day, and I can promise you that you will look and feel 100% better—not only about yourself, but towards others too. I remember a line from a song many years ago that stated: "take a look at yourself, and you will see others differently," and it's oh, so true. Good luck, and may life be yours for the taking!

The key to staying connected to change, both on and off the job, is to S.T.O.P. See The Opportunity and Permit it to happen. However, this can only happen if we realize we have been given the abilities to do so.

—Rosita

Change Is All There Is…

God Grant me the serenity to accept the things I cannot change, courage to change the things I can, and wisdom to know the difference. This verse was instilled in my head from the time I was a young child. It was mounted in a frame and hung on a wall above our kitchen table. Each time I sat at that table I would read it over and over again; eventually I memorized it, but I really didn't understand what it truly meant until I became an adult and started out on my own in life.

I understand now that the "wisdom to know the difference" holds a powerful meaning. It is that critical component that can either make us or break us, in a life filled with ongoing changes, challenges, and adjustments. Regardless of whether we are dealing with personal change by choice, circumstances beyond our control, or the inevitable changes that constantly occur in our work environments, we can minimize the impact of the change by understanding and accepting what we *can* and *cannot control.* The one thing that we can control is ourselves, in terms of how we react to and deal with any type of change or challenge. Change is an opportunity for us to show off our emotional and mental "Top Guns" and to demonstrate to the world what we are really made of on the inside.

Over the past decade we have had to come to terms with incredible changes both on and off the job. Technology has unveiled itself in new and advanced forms and has invaded our lives through the use of cell phones, e-mails, laptops, etc. Most of us stay in the "ON" mode and never shut down. Our technological gadgets that we thought would slow the pace down, have actually done quite the opposite.

We have also had to accept the reality that job security is a thing of the past, and that the days of working nine to five, and retiring after twenty-five years with the gold watch, just don't exist anymore. Those were the good ol' days, or were they? Yes, things have changed, and will continue to change, because change is never over, it's the very fabric of our existence.

The reality of the workplace today is that we must now "bring ourselves to work," which means relying upon all of our internal resources as our new source of security. We must constantly look for the hidden opportunities in our changing environments, and take advantage of them, knowing that we have the abilities to adapt. We must also stay connected to change so that we are aware of the impact it is having on our health and our relationships with others, both on and off the job. Finally, we must take time to consider how any type of change is in keeping with our core values and principals. This is critical because if we find ourselves compromising either of them, it may be a clear signal that it is time for us to move on.

How are you weathering the changes that are occurring in your workplace? The chart on the following page depicts a *fun* but informative analysis of how I perceived participants were feeling in regards to the changes occurring in their places of work. This information was gathered just through informal conversation with my participants during my presentations on change management and self-care as a professional speaker.

Your Personal Weather Forecast

Great Weather

You are definitely feeling no pain. Nothing ever gets you down. Even if it does, you bounce back in record time. In your opinion, change is not the enemy. You see this time as one of opportunity. You're high on self-esteem and may in fact be high on something else as well...

Sprinkling of Rain

You have felt the impact. You have great survival skills. You feel confident that if you just remain positive and rely on your incredible refueling resources, you will be just fine.

Light Shower Activity

You are like the guy caught in the rain without his umbrella. You definitely feel the impact (you're wet). However, you won't forget your umbrella next time. You will keep both this tool and the many other tools and skills you have within reach. You welcome change in a positive manner. You feel the loss, but you pick yourself up, dry yourself off, and begin moving forward.

Heavy Rain

Things are starting to become a little uncomfortable for you. You're not panicking yet, but you feel unsure about the forecast for the next little while. You're coping with the pressure, but it seems as if it's always one thing after another. You could use a break!

Monsoon

You have been left nearly drowning. You have a slight sickness called the "poor me syndrome." This rain has hit you hard. You have had no time to plan. You were waiting patiently for the"gold watch and handshake, so that you could retire peacefully. Your frustration, negativity, and your "how dare they do this to me attitude" is guiding you toward a slow suicide.

"Hurricane"

You are truly ticked off at the world and would like to drop a bomb on the perpetrators. You fly off the handle easily. You often feel out of control. You have difficulty focusing and see change as the enemy. You cause emotional havoc wherever you go. You are an accident waiting to happen. You have been married to your job forever. This divorce is getting messy!!

81

All Aboard the Change Train...

Do You Have Your Ticket?

Being aboard the "change train" means making the adjust-ments necessary to stay sane, by working with what is, rather than with what used to be. This requires that we make a com-mitment and develop a plan of action which will allow us to move forward and meet the new workplace demands head-on. Your boarding pass is guaranteed once you can walk your way through and embrace the following steps. It's important that you get on board and stay on board; otherwise the systems will reject you.

Step 1: Understand the following five simple truths about change:

- Change is at the very fabric of our existence. People and orga-nizations are constantly changing. The way you run an organi-zation will have to constantly be examined and re-defined.

- Change is about revising and updating to meet the current political, social, and economical environment.

- Change is not the enemy.

- Change is an opportunity for a breakthrough not a breakdown!

- Change is never done. When you're through changing, you're through....

Step 2: Engage in a personal revolution; control the controllable (self).

FACT: Did you know that when situations are changing, the most important resource that you need to assess, rely on, and manage is yourself? *Answer the following questions truthfully. This is how we start the process of dealing with change from the inside out. It will also help us to determine our emotional and mental readiness to managing change.*

Self Assessment:

- __Who am I? What am I about? What is my purpose?
- Am I doing soulful work?
- Am I caring for myself emotionally, mentally, and spiritually?
- What attracted me to this position?
- Why did I choose to work here?
- Why do I continue to work here?
- What am I sacrificing by working here and trying to maintain the status quo?
- Can I work differently now, or am I stuck in a time warp?
- Is there an issue much bigger than the upheaval in the workplace that has me stuck, and if so, what am I prepared to do to become 'unstuck'?
- Do I love what I do?
- Am I passionate about the mission, goals, and objectives of the organization that I work for, and are they in keeping with my personal values?
- Is there a balance between my personal life and my home life?
- Am I capable of making a graceful exit if necessary?
- How do I refuel each day?

Step 3: Utilize Your Personal Safety Net.

Attitude: Your attitude is your most prized possession; what is yours worth?

Skills, Talents, and Abilities: When we view change as an opportunity instead of a curse, a wonderful self-revelation takes place. It's amazing what you will find out.

Energy/Enthusiasm: How is your energy level? Embracing the new takes far less energy then hanging on to the past.

Self-esteem: Are you high on self-esteem? Without it you are nothing!

Dream Power: Do you have dreams? What are you doing about them? A dream without a goal will always be just a dream.

Ability to laugh: Do you still own the gift of laughter? Injecting humour into our lives has health benefits, increases productivity and creativity, and gives the heart a workout equivalent to three minutes of strenuous rowing (Dr. William Fry Jr., Stanford Medical University).

P.M.S: (Personal Mission Statement.)

Hope & Faith: believe and you will achieve!

Step 4: Understand and deal with the new workplace realities:

- You are much more than your job description. Do not define yourself solely by your job.

- The most important question that you must ask yourself every-day of our work life is: "What am I becoming?"

- Accept the notion that job security is a thing of the past. The only real security you can depend on is recognizing your own skills, talents, and abilities and having the courage to utilize them.

If you can grasp these four simple truths, then you are now ready to get on board the Change Train, and take a ride filled with endless possibilities and opportunities. Your task now is to develop a simple plan of action that will allow you to stay on board and connected to change, in a healthy and productive way.

The aging process is a blessing, not a curse. The ongoing molding and remolding of the human heart, soul, spirit and psyche, is a miracle in action. The changes are simply reminders of where we've been, and they are to be worn as badges of honour.

—*Rosita*

Mother Time Is a Friend of Mine...

Featuring an Unauthorized Blurb on Barbie—the Doll

"Mother Time" is a friend of mine, a faithful partner since the beginning of time. Like a sculptor creating his great work of art, she meticulously molds and remolds my inner and physical beauty to keep it in line with my years. She has taught me through her creative process that aging is nothing to fear.

Why are we so obsessed with the thought of aging? Why do we dye and lie? Why do we suck and tuck?

Been on a diet lately? Still squeezing that size twelve butt into the size eight jeans you wore a decade ago? Still washing that grey right out of your hair? Still using that wrinkle-free lotion? Does it work? Still living with the fantasy that you can make time stand still? If you answered yes to just one of these questions, then you need to get a firm grip on this News Flash—*Mother Time doesn't put the aging process on hold*. Her role is to keep us in touch with reality, and to help us age gracefully and elegantly.

Why won't we let Mother Time do her duty? Why can't we let her stay the course, and age us gracefully and elegantly? Why must we always stop her in her tracks and chastise her because she paints mystical laugh lines around our mouths, beautifully crafts sand bags below our eyes, and oh, how she delicately paints streaks of silver and grey into our hair; and if she's so inclined, she'll even relieve you of your duties of ever having to own a comb again as you now become the proud owner of a look very similar to a bowling ball. Oh, but she doesn't stop there—she unveils all of her creative juices when she allows the skin to stretch so elegantly, and the muscles to go on an extended vacation. The best part is those little dimples that sneak out from under our shorts in the summer (alias "fat.") All of these create a most interesting, but beautiful, change in our physiques. Only Mother Time has the ability to master a craft so delicate in nature, and remold it over and over again in such an honest fashion. You see, my friends, she can only sculpt the truth—and the truth of the matter is that the changes we will face emotionally, mentally and physically are inevitable because they are all a part of life.

One of my most memorable moments with Mother Time on a physical level occurred when she remolded my gluteus maximus into something very similar to gluteus Jell-O. Imagine, maximus one day, Jell-O the next; but that's exactly how it happened. Well sort of.... I suppose if I were to be really honest with myself, this molding process would have had to have started some time ago. There's no way that it could have been done all in one day's work. I was just too busy to notice her fine efforts, until one morning when I was getting dressed for work. When I looked into the mirror, to my surprise, my bum had literally dropped. I was simply amazed. I'll never forget the look on my colleagues' faces when I made a grand entrance into work that same day and announced, "My bum dropped." I could tell by the expressions on their faces that they were not sure if they should laugh or comfort me.

At that moment of awakening, I realized that Mother Time was a powerful sculptor and change agent, who was here to stay. You see, one of the most honorable qualities about Mother Time is that she is a very faithful follower, and has been from the very start. She embraced us from the moment we were conceived, and not once has she ever deceived us. She's always been right on schedule, at each interval of our physical and emotional development.

Mother Time knows exactly what she is doing. She is an artist who has taken great lessons from God. Our emotional health also affects our aging process. How then did we ever become a nation of exhausted, stressed out, 'achy breaky hearts'? Are we completely out of touch with the whole notion of self and self-care? Not caring for ourselves emotionally, mentally, physically, and spiritually can wreak havoc on our lives. The sad shape of our heart, soul, and physical well-being is painting telltale lines and bulges all over our bodies. That's our work of art, not the work of Mother Time. Unresolved anger, frustration, stress, etc. are part of the reason why we both age, and sometimes die, before our time.

Mother Time must also compete with our obsession to be perfect, like the models we see on those magazines placed strategically at the check-out counters in many stores. You know the ones with the flawless features and a look that says: "In addition to being physically perfect, I'm also emotionally and mentally flawless."

And as if that's not enough interference for Mother Time to deal with, along comes this rejuvenated, awesomely-equipped little babe that throws a powerful curve ball that even the best can't contend with. She graces the shelf of every store that has a toy section, and unlike the supermodels, she just seems to go on forever.

Every little girl begs for her company and many women secretly want a life like hers, mainly because of her bod. I'm talking about a young thing created by Mrs. and Mr. Ruth and Elliot Handler on March 9, 1959 (my gosh, the same year I was born) that's had a major impact on our relationship with the beautiful Mother Time. Her name is Barbara Millicent Roberts, better known as the Barbie doll.

We can't completely blame the supermodels, or in particular Barbie, for our obsession to be ageless. While their influence has played a major role and still remains a great influence, it's time for us to get over our obsessions with youthfulness, and get a firm grip on reality. Take Barbie, for example. Did you not clue into the secrets of her ageless life even after the Danish group Aqua wrote a song about Barbie, in which Barbie herself sings: "I'm a Barbie girl in a Barbie world; life in plastic, it's fantastic."

The key word here is plastic, as in *not real!* I'll say it again, she is not real! Barbie can sit and eat all the bonbons and Twinkies she wants, and her hips won't move an inch. She's a perfectly well-packaged, stress-free, fat-free, acne-free, ageless teen doll, that will probably live forever in her plastic world. As for us, well, we are well-packaged in our own fantastic way too, except we don't realize it because we haven't embraced Mother Time yet.

So let Barbie stay in her fantastic plastic world. Let's not breathe so much life into her. So what if she never ages and is able to maintain that fantastic body forever? Maybe the creators knew exactly what they were doing when they created Barbie. Like Adam and Eve in their entire splendour, they were defeated by the serpent. Perhaps she was created to tempt us into believing that we aren't really beautiful and that life is better in the plastic world. If that's the case, I think its working.

Aging is a normal process. It is not a curse. It is a necessary blessing in life, and it doesn't make us *old* men and *old* women; it makes us *older* men and *older* women. It wasn't Mother Time that came up with the term "old age." In fact, if we would just take a moment to embrace Mother Time and appreciate her fine work, we would realize that her sculpting of our physical and emotional self throughout the years, if left unhampered, actually depicts a new age—in fact, a new beginning, a new era, a time to celebrate yet another milestone in our journey of life. It's not a time to become desperate, uptight, and pleading with Mother Time to slow down the process. The process has always been slow. It was when we became threatened by the idea of aging and came up with our own stay-youthful schemes, that we started messing up the great work of Mother Time. But being the faithful missionary that she is, she always keeps stride despite our loyalties to the stay-young schemes.

You see, the aging process is simply life. *Change, aging, life, growth; they all go hand in hand.* Did you really think you would look exactly the same at fifty as you did at twenty-five? Fat chance!! (Pardon the pun.) What I would like to know is: who decided that sixty was old—or forty for that matter? Better still, who decided that "over the hill" refers to the fifty-plus population? What exactly does "over the hill" mean anyway? I don't get it. Furthermore, who decided that only women in their early twenties could wear tank tops and 'Daisy Duke' shorts, sending the barely thirty-something women into a frenzy, and wondering if their bodies and mental state would ever be the same again.

When you reach a certain age, whatever that might be, and feel that you're over the hill, that's probably because that's your perspective on life. Others, and there are many, will view it completely differently, and look forward to a new chapter of life with all its mysteries. Seeing the aging process from a negative or desperate position, is a coward's way of viewing a reality that cannot be ignored. If you are that uptight about aging, then there is probably a wound deeper than just the issue of aging.

Aging doesn't just start happening at a designated age set by our society. The aging process started from the moment you were conceived. Remember a thing called birthdays? No matter how old you are chronologically, and no matter how many grey hairs you can count on your head, in your ears or in your nose, the real truth about your age can only be determined by the shape of your heart and your soul at any given time in your life. It is also measured by the friendships we keep, the young children's hearts we touch, the flowers we smell, how much we appreciate life and all the beauty around us, how we appreciate silence, laughter, and the songs in our hearts. It's no secret that life is a continuous journey with many peaks, hills, and valleys. Throughout life, we will probably go over many hills, so why is going over the hill so different because you turn fifty? Is this the last hill? Is there nothing left of the journey now? Do you suddenly fall into an abyss?

I bet that the term "over the hill" was invented by someone who needed a serious attitude adjustment; either that, or by someone with a great sense of humor, and if that's the case: chill out, people!

Let's start carrying the torch for our hearts and souls and our physical well-being right now at this very moment. Let's not wait until we are in such a state of disrepair that the panic button goes off, and suddenly we become paranoid about the shape of our buttocks and our battle-weary hearts and souls. You see, Mother Time does stay the course, and when we interfere she cannot undo what we've done to ourselves. Lack of care for the inner and outer self will cause the body to age quicker and in a not-so-fashionable way. Remember, Mother Time ages us gracefully. All she asks of us, is to respect her work and take care of ourselves. If we don't, Mother Time won't pick up the broken pieces. She just continues on with her journey.

How much we appreciate her work depends on us as individuals. Most people who are caring for themselves embrace Mother Time because they are high on self-esteem, feel great about themselves, and welcome what life has to offer. They haven't been tripped up by Barbie and all the other non-reality based distractions. The hair loss, the wrinkles, the reshaped buns, the graying hair, the stretch marks, and the molding and remolding of our emotional well-being are simply reminders of where we've been, and they are badges of honour, not despair. Wear yours proudly!

Take time every day to do something fun for yourself and/or with someone you love. At the end of the day, replay those moments and smile.

—*Rosita*

User Friendly Tips for Creating a Funtastic Work Environment

This was no time for play. This was no time for fun. This was no time for games. There was work to be done (Excerpt from *The Cat in the Hat*).

—*Dr. Seuss*

Does this sound like your work environment? If so, it's time to lighten up and start enjoying work. Many of us spend more time at our places of work then we do with our families or significant others. If that's the case, we'd better find some ways to lighten the load emotionally and mentally. I've heard many people say: "I'm dying to have fun," but I've never heard of anyone dying from having fun. Yes, you can have fun, and still get the job done!

❑ Let your office space be a reflection of who you are. If it's dull and boring, that is how people will perceive you. Put some life and energy into your workspace. You will feel energized immediately. Add some fun pictures, toys etc. Spice it up with some color.

❑ Drive co-workers nuts with your cheerfulness. Nuts is better then cranky and uninteresting, and it does wonders for your immune system.

❑ Take sanity breaks; designate a certain cubicle/office as the 'give-me-a-break' room, a special therapeutic room armed with toys, surprises, silly gadgets, funny videos, and good eats! Let people know that this is a room where negativity is not welcomed, and only those in need of a good time can enter. It can be your one-stop re-fuelling shop.

❑ Have fun music playing in your office! Something that will make people want to get up and dance. There is nothing wrong with a little "hip shaking" in the office if it's done in good taste. If you are not in environments that will allow music, then carry a tune in your head and start shaking it!

❑ Get some fun pens, posters, and mugs in the office.

❑ Have a 'take-a-geek-to-lunch' day. Post your geekiest picture outside your office door! Have a contest and vote on the geek who will be treated to lunch by his/her peers. Do this once a month.

❑ Use your time in the washroom well. Ensure that each stall is stacked with funny magazines or material to read. (Why not buy some fun toilet paper?) Using the washroom really can provide relief.

❑ Create guardian angels in your workplace. Place everyone's name in a hat, and you become a secret guardian angel to the person whose name you draw. Surprise them once in a while with something special when it appears that they could use a little boost, or perhaps just before a meeting they might be nervous about attending.

❑ Check out your library at home and at work. Does it include fun books? Say goodbye to self-help books that convince us that we are ego-starved and needy.

Special Note: These same tips can be implemented in your home environment as well. Spice up the rooms in your home that you use most. Look at the type of magazines and books you have laying around. Have fun music playing, and don't forget to dance once in awhile.

And Now the Choice Is Yours…

Each of us is but one person, minuscule in comparison to the rest of the world; yet we all play an incredibly significant role in how the universe unfolds itself each day.

Our attitudes, our thoughts, gestures, behaviors, choices we make or don't make, and how and what we communicate, will in some way affect other people. What message do you send out to the universe each day? Is it one of positive hope and inspiration?

I believe that there is a strong correlation between the messages that the universe receives from us each day, and the shape of our hearts, souls, and physical well-being. I hope that I have communicated how important it is to know oneself, the gifts we have to give, the importance of taking care of ourselves, and capturing what really matters in this wonderful life that has been given to us. More importantly, I hope that I have emphasized that we only have a short time in which to embrace life and serve our purpose.

I believe that each of us was put on this earth to serve a particular purpose, and that many of us have yet to discover that. Not knowing our purpose, and who we are, often leaves us unprepared for the unexpected changes and challenges that we will face in our lives, both on and off the job. I hope that by reading my book you have been encouraged to look deep inside of yourself, to discover all that you truly are, and to use your God-given talents in a way that will add value, not only to your life, but to the lives of all those you will touch in a lifetime.

My purpose has been clearly communicated to me by God— and it is *to spread the good news about joyful and healthy living, and to connect soulfully, lovingly, and spiritually with the rest of the world.* If I can do this in accordance with His will, then my living will not be in vain. I will have left my mark.

We have a choice as to how we start each day, and how we react to any given situation in a day. We can choose to feel motivated, hopeful, and inspired or we can choose to be the opposite. If it is a choice that is *not* nurturing to our hearts and souls, then we start the disease process, and our bodies advance one step forward in the direction of our demise.

The attitude we climb out of bed with each morning will be the very foundation we will be dependent upon throughout the day. It's that same foundation that will affect not only your day, but those around you. How do you start each day? Is it one built on a solid foundation of positive affirmation, self-regard and energy, so that you can access and rely on your awesomely-equipped internal resources as your pillars of strength? This is what we need in order to deal with a day filled with adversity, challenges, and the unexpected. Or is your foundation one that falters and provides no support at any given point in the day because it's built on lack of nurturance and negative energy?

The choice is yours; which one will it be? I found my answer to this question many years ago, and my life has never been the same. My spirit has been set free; I feel at peace with myself and the universe. I know through experience and with the deepest of convictions, that life can be whatever you paint it to be. I trust that you will choose to paint yours filled with hope, faith, and happiness, because you truly deserve it!

God bless you all,
Rosita

Somewhere...

Somewhere deep inside my soul there lies a special "me"
She's ready to reveal herself for all the world to see.
She spreads her wings, they open wide, so daring, she takes flight
To leave behind the storms of her past, for the dawning of new light.

The storms of past are simply this: times that used to be;
The good, the bad, the ugly, but they are all a part of "me";
And the wind beneath her wings will be the memories that she'll keep;
And the others she will lay to rest, forever they must sleep.

She soars up high on courage and hope, her heart and soul they
see the light,
No more: "wish I may, or wish I might; have no more tearful and
sleepless nights."
The here and now they embrace her warmly, she dances no more
with the past,
This bird has found direction now, her life is changing fast.

She no longer plays host to the *storms of past*, no longer will she
live in fear,
She just simply spreads her angelic wings when trouble is brewing
near.
The *storms of past* they don't like this, they cannot take defeat,
But she is stronger now, she knows their game, she wins each time
they meet.

Rosita Hall

She's a survivor of the *storms of past,* she's confronted her ghosts, now she is free.
That part of her life has turned to dust; now new beginnings are all she can see.
And through her eyes the truth is revealed, of a life she's so bravely endured,
And her faith, her friends, and her zest for life, now keep her self-assured.

So the magic dances in her feet, and her heart overflows with love
Look up above, see her in flight, she's like a mourning dove.
Oh, the *freeing* up of the heart and soul, is a wonderful sight to see;
Life in the *present moment,* is a place where all hearts should be.

So she embraces her faith that keeps her in flight
High above all the rubbish, what a beautiful sight;
Spreading love over darkness, and helping others to see
That we need closure and courage, in order to be free.

She treasures this life that through God's love she's achieved
Now she has been given a reason to forever believe,
That no matter the weather or how ugly the storm,
God gave us our wings on the day we were born.

—Rosita Hall

Reclaiming Their Lives…

How do you mend a broken heart, shattered dreams, broken promises, and a spirit that has been beaten to the ground and left lying aimlessly on unclaimed grounds, while people knowingly and unknowingly walk upon it?

This book wouldn't be complete if I didn't dedicate this chapter to the thousands of women and their children who courageously gathered the strength to pick themselves up, dust off their shattered egos, and rebuild their lives—a task that only those with sheer hope, faith, and determination could ever afford to do, emotionally, mentally, and physically. Within these few short paragraphs lies a message for all of us no matter what our circumstances, and it's simply this: "Faith is the daring of the soul to go further than it can see" (*William Newton Clark*).

Over the past twenty years in my role as a Social Worker, my own faith was often challenged, and my heart ached deeply as I witnessed the silent teardrops of my colleagues each time another battered woman sat down to tell her story. It ate away at my emotions and disturbed me deeply, and at times made me question whether or not there were any good men left on the face of this earth. However, each night as I took my hiatus from work, and went home to be with my husband, my faith would be restored over and over again, and just to make sure that it stayed intact, God blessed me with two angelic sons.

I have now concluded that there are no bad people in this world, just people who have been led astray, and who have not been taught how to deal with their own personal wars raging from within.

Men who abuse their intimate partners have been taught, and in many ways, have been given permission to act in an aggressive and an abusive way. It's all about control. So when I was able to come to terms with this, I focused my attention on helping women reclaim their power and take back control over their lives.

It wasn't about trying to fix their partners, or to make him change, or about who was to blame. Blame is not the issue. The only person we can fix is ourselves. To me, it made more sense to teach women to control the controllable. Given the right direction and support, we can all control our actions and the decisions we make. However, in order to do so, we must first reclaim the *self*.

Reclaiming *self* means taking total responsibility for making the necessary changes that will give us back our self-respect and self-esteem, and keep us out of unhealthy relationships.

While acknowledging the pain, and being able to talk about their feelings of being hurt, cheated, and robbed was critical, the real journey started when these women would re-surface beyond all of that garbage; rebuild, and make a fresh start—and that's exactly what I was able to witness over and over again from so many women.

I watched emphatically as women began renovating their personal havens. In the beginning, it was always a struggle, because the past is a powerful demon, and many women had trouble coming to the surface long enough to see that there was a whole world and a future waiting for them. The catch however, was that they had to be hungry for a new life, and they had to get out of the grips of the past. They had to try on their renewed self-esteem and self-respect, and begin the journey.

The task, although not an easy one, took time, but together we always made good progress, and I've seen so many lives change and I often wondered by the end of a counselling term if I was even dealing with the same person. The transformation I witnessed was simply incredible.

You know how it is in the winter time when you look out your window. You see nothing but empty branches, and all those plants that were once so radiant, alive, colorful, and growing, lie stagnant and lifeless; and then suddenly, the miracle unfolds itself with the spring's love. Well, that's what it was like with the women I worked with. Miracles happened right in front of my eyes, as women would rise to the occasion and come to life again.

Their spring was their ability to silence the demons and let their self-esteem, self-courage, and self-respect take over. Many of us have had wintry periods in our lives through losses, sicknesses, and family issues that have knocked us down for the count, but it's important that we remember that spring will come again with courage.

The following is a poem I wrote about a woman named Tracey, who had a story and a past that even I had to convince myself she could get through.

As I journeyed with Tracey through her past, from the time she was a very young girl when the abuse began, and into her young adulthood where it continued from all those who claimed to love her, I had to really dig deep into my bag of counselling techniques to convince her that true love does indeed exist. I'll never forget the day she asked me to describe to her my relationship with my husband because she had no idea what a true and loving relationship was all about. When I finished describing my relationship with my husband to her, she still wasn't convinced that such a relationship existed, at least not here on planet Earth. To say the least, Tracey had a lot of work to do, but she was so desperate to begin a new life, even though it scared the heck out of her.

The one thing Tracey realized early in the process was that she had to meet her "devils" face-to-face in order to move on, and that she could then find her courage from within to keep her afloat. I worked with Tracey for more than a year, and we remained in contact with each other for about a year after that. Tears come to my eyes when I think about what this woman was able to do, to finally get to know herself. Tracey went the full ten rounds with her demons and won by a knockout. Her heart and soul have been set free. The journey within is about how Tracey freed herself by connecting with, and utilizing, her resources from within!

The Inner Journey

The stairway to Heaven, I've been told, is waiting above for me;
It's trimmed in gold and silver lace, and the doorway is marked "I'm free."
Somehow I can envision that place, the land that the living call "free";
But for now, I am here, inside I must climb to the stairway to Heaven in me!

The abuse has left its emotional toll, death nearly welcomed me in;
For inside I was dying a painful death, but self-love welcomed me in.
And to this day I cannot explain how self-love emerged in me,
But it conquered my pain and showed me the way, to a stairway to heaven in me!

My stairway to Heaven is trimmed with courage, and was built especially for me,
And when my past attempts to haunt me, it whispers "follow me…"
Deep down the winding staircase, and through the internal gate,
My soulful friends they greet me; they never hesitate.

They dance, they sing a joyful song, their laughter comforts me,
They journey deep within my heart, their message loud and clear
My soul cries out, "She needs you," and my daring friends begin;
Joy shouts out, "I am with you"; my courage gives a grin,
Self-esteem and love embrace me, my Heaven is here within!!

Rosita Hall

My message here is simple, as clear as it can be:
Self-love is a powerful weapon for its strength has rescued me.
So now I know the meaning when the world cries out to me;
Heaven is that peaceful place the living call "free."

—Rosita Hall
November 9, 1998